St Andrews Castle

by **Stewart Cruden** OBE ARIBA FSA
formerly Inspector of Ancient Monuments
for Scotland

Edinburgh
Her Majesty's Stationery Office

1. *The entrance and fore tower*

Palace, Fortress and Prison

The Castle as seen today is principally the work of the sixteenth century but overlies and incorporates within its walls parts of earlier work. Documentary evidence indicates that the first castle was erected *circa* 1200 by Bishop Roger as a residence for himself and his successors of greater and more appropriate distinction than was hitherto provided in the priory. From its foundation the castle was intimately connected with the cathedral dignitaries whose charge it was, and in the course of time served the threefold purpose of episcopal palace, fortress and state prison.

The Wars of Independence

The castle suffered in the ebb and flow of fortune during the Wars of Independence, was captured and re-captured, dismantled and rebuilt by both Scots and English. In the spring of 1303 or 1304 preparations were made in it for the accommodation of Edward I and his Queen, Margaret. Shortly after Bannockburn, the English having lost it with other fortresses in southern Scotland, it was occupied and repaired by Bishop William Lamberton (1298–1328) 'a clerk of gret fame and vertue', once Chancellor in the Cathedral of Glasgow and a dauntless patriot and stubborn opponent of Edward.

Again, however, it fell into English hands, during the weak resistance of David II to the aggressive activities of the pretender Balliol on behalf of Edward III. It was rebuilt in 1336 by two English Lords, De Beaumont and De Ferrers, who are also credited with the rebuilding of the now vanished Leuchars Castle in the same year.

In 1337, to quote two chronicles of the later Middle Ages, Sir Andrew Moray, Warden of Scotland, 'got to St. Andrews and with his engines mightily besieged the castle thereof for three weeks' . . . 'and to the erd syn dang it doun', an example of deliberate demolition or scorched earth policy effected by Bruce and other Scots leaders during the uncertain days of the wars against the English, when a Scottish stronghold of one month might be an English base of operation in the next.

The Castle and the Stewarts

For about fifty years after that the castle lay neglected and in ruins until the succession to the Bishopric of Walter Traill (1385–1401) who, to quote Fordun, the fourteenth-century chronicler, 'died in the castle of St Andrews which he himself had erected from its foundations'. In it James I, previous to his captivity in England, was educated by Bishop Wardlaw (1403–1440), who founded the University and to whom James returned in 1425 to make the castle his residence, attracted no doubt by the well-known capabilities and hospitality of his erstwhile tutor. Here Bishop Kennedy demonstrated to James II his method of breaking the growing power of the nobles, as he would a sheaf of arrows, by separating them and breaking them singly. There is reason to believe from a reference in the so-called 'Golden Charter' of James II that his son James III was born in the castle in 1451. During his reign it was the palace and prison of Patrick Graham, first Archbishop of St Andrews, before his continual confinement in Iona, the abbey of

2. The castle in 1718. After an engraving by Captain John Slezer

Dunfermline and the island of St Serf in Lochleven, where he died and was buried in 1478.

Further ironic episodes in the dramatic history of this castle occurred after the death of Archbishop Alexander Stewart at Flodden in 1513. The See was contended for by four Scottish competitors: Gavin Douglas, who took possession of the castle; Prior John Hepburn of St Andrews, who drove him out and manned both castle and cathedral 'with men, weapons and artillery'; James Beaton, Archbishop of Glasgow, who eventually held the office; and Andrew Forman, Bishop of Moray, who was elected. During the interval Douglas the poet retired from the field. He was soon after imprisoned by the Regent in the very castle he had good reason to believe would have been his episcopal palace. He was subsequently elected to the Bishopric of Dunkeld.

Archbishop and Cardinal Beaton

The next history that can be ascertained is of the period of Archbishop James Beaton, the above-mentioned, who held his office from 1523–1539, during which time the castle maintained such great splendour and lavish hospitality that this was commented upon by the English ambassador in the following terms: 'I understand there hath not been such a house kept in Scotland many days before, as of late the said archbishop hath kept, and yet keepeth; insomuch as at the being with him of these lords, (Angus, Lennox, Argyle, etc), both horses and men, he gave livery nightly to twenty-one score horses.'

James Beaton was succeeded by his nephew, the celebrated Cardinal David Beaton (1539–1546), a man of strong Catholic ambitions. He incurred the wrath of Henry VIII by refusing to ratify the marriage contract proposed by Henry for his son Edward with the infant Mary, daughter of James V. Determined to unite the countries with his blessings, by force if not by matrimony, Henry declared war on Scotland in 1543.

While the Cardinal in 1546 was causing the fortifications of the castle to be strengthened against a threatened attack, the garrison was simply, quietly and effectively overcome by a stratagem of a few Protestant adherents who

3. *The fore tower*

entered the castle with the masons employed on the work and thus gained unopposed admittance and possession before the inmates were astir. The Cardinal was then murdered, and his body hung from a wallhead, not three months after he had watched from a window the torments of George Wishart burning for heresy. 'Incontinent, they brought the Cardinal dead to the wall-head in a pair of sheets, and hung him over the wall by the tane arm and the tane foot, and bade the people see their god'.

The Protestants, with assistance from Henry, held out for a year until the besieging forces were augmented by a French fleet under the command of the Prior of Capua – the Scots under the regency of Mary of Guise having turned towards the French for assistance – and the castle fell, not before it had been sadly damaged by gun-fire directed from the college steeple and the wall-tops of the abbey church. The castle garrison, including John Knox and others who had sought refuge in the troubled days before the siege began, were taken away by the French. Knox was a galley-slave for the next two years.

Cardinal Beaton's successor was Archbishop John Hamilton (1549–1571). He is known to have rebuilt the castle and his armorial device, a five-pointed star, or cinquefoil, may be seen on the work he did, above the present entrance, and on a heraldic panel between the two large windows of the Fore Tower.

The subsequent history of the castle is less spectacular and largely one of changing ownership without wars and siege. In 1587, during the Presbyterian ascendancy, the Act of Annexation was passed which transferred the castle, along with other church property, to the Crown. In 1606 it was granted by James VI to the Earl of Dunbar. In 1612 it reverted to the Archbishopric. After this period its importance gradually diminished and the Town Council in 1654 ordered part of the fabric to be used for the repair of the harbour walls. In 1911 the monument was taken into custody and guardianship.

Building History

It is not improbable that the earliest masonry existing is part of the castle of *c.* 1200. Although there are no moulding or features by which it can be closely dated, its general characteristics, large well-dressed stones, laid in courses with narrow joints, are quite in keeping with early thirteenth-century style and practice. The castle is reputed to have been founded in 1200. We know it was occupied and repaired by Bishop Lamberton at the beginning of the fourteenth century. By bringing the architectural evidence into close relationship with the historical we cannot easily reject the evidence for this dating as a point of departure. This building is represented today by the cross-wall which divides the Fore Tower into two compartments, with a small extent of side walling adjacent to it on either side (see plan).

The next period represented appears to be the 1336 rebuilding. At this time the early castle, which would have been a simple rectangular tower perhaps with an adjacent courtyard defended by a palisade and ditch, must have been enlarged. The tower seems to have been extended in both directions, northwards and southwards. Of this building, demolished by Andrew Moray in 1337, there remains in the Fore Tower only the five lowest quoins at its south-west angle and the fifteen at the south-east along with the corresponding courses of the east face and the evidence of the entrance on the south front. These indications of distinctive masonry are even more apparent in the interior where the masonry of this period is noticeably superior to the masonry elsewhere in the castle. On the west side the courses include the jambs of a cross-loop of fourteenth-century type now blocked up by the later south range. At the south these courses include the jambs and springings of the entrance and at the east the jambs of the postern gate, curtailed in the sixteenth century into a window with a gun-loop below the sill.

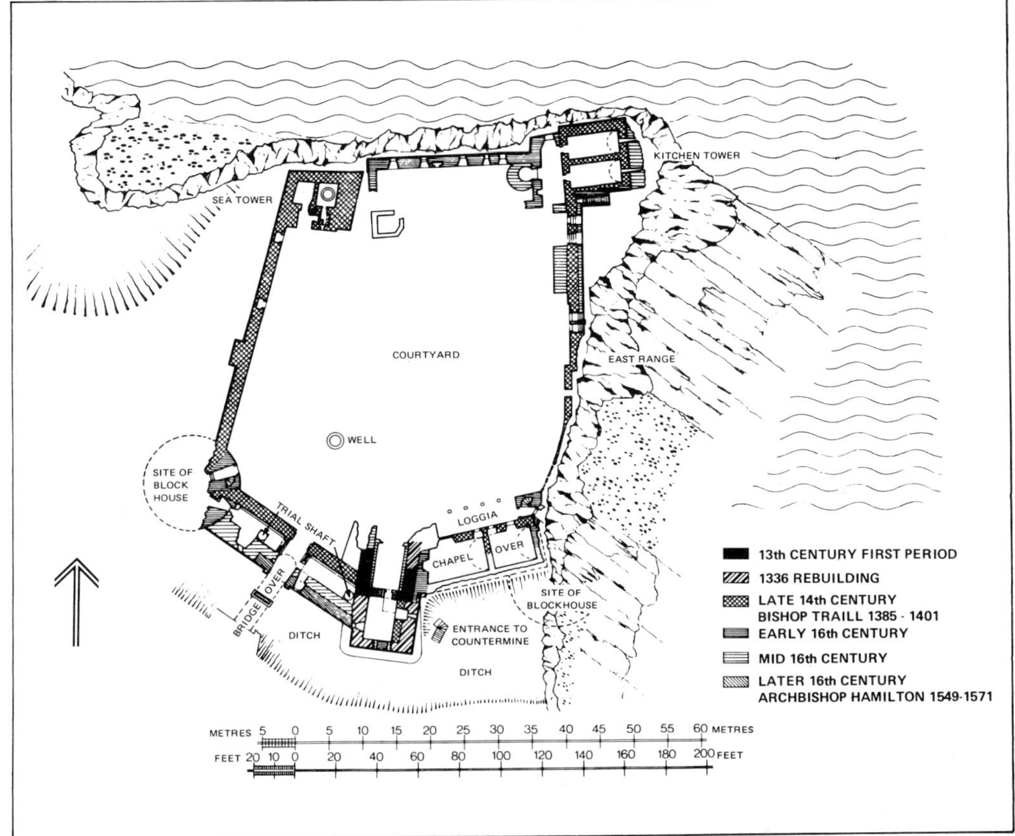

During the period of Traill (1385–1401) the castle was again repaired. He repaired the Fore Tower and erected curtain walls all round the site, of which the south-west and west are substantially represented today, the former as the inner wall of the existing front range, as described below. He also built the Sea Tower and Kitchen Tower of which the lower existing parts are his work: the upper parts were rebuilt in the fifteenth or sixteenth century. In the early sixteenth century rose the circular Blockhouses at the south-east and south-west corners, but they survived only a short time before the siege, bombardment, and destruction of the castle in 1546–47. The last building period traceable is of the later sixteenth century – the restoration work of Cardinal Beaton's successor, Archbishop Hamilton, after the great siege. He erected the present handsome frontal range.

Chambers overlooking the sea

The castle is protected on the north and east by the cliffs and sea which, on the east side particularly, were more distant than at present. Martin, writing in 1683, state that 'in his time there were people still living who remembered seeing bowls played on the level ground to the east and north', and Grose in 1791, quoting old writings, says that the proprietor of a neighbouring estate 'had the privilege of driving his cattle and goods on the east side of the castle, which for some centuries past no man could have done'.

On the south and west, the castle was cut off by a deep ditch, the approach to the tower being by a drawbridge. A map of St Andrews of *c*. 1534 shows a gatehouse to the south with an arched entrance to the castle precincts.

The Entrance and Fore Tower

It is appropriate to mention at this point that the present entrance is the fourth. The original to the castle is now incorporated in and hidden by the great southern tower known as the Fore Tower, being in the cross-wall that divides the tower into two compartments. This cross-wall was then the outside wall of an original tower and the narrow opening in it is the shrunken remains of the first great entrance gateway. The second gateway was brought forward when the tower was extended and can be seen, partially blocked up, in the south wall of the tower. The door jambs of this entrance are exposed beside the later walling which blocked it when the approach was transferred to the western frontal range. The jambs are boldly chamfered, provided with chases in the masonry to house the portcullis, and rebated for a two-leafed door.

5. The Mine

Above the entrance is one of the two 'rainures' or vertical slots for the gaffs of the drawbridge. The other would be in a corresponding position, now built up, on the west side of the large upper window. This type of drawbridge with gaffs does not commonly occur before the fourteenth century. This entrance ws 0.9 m lower than its predecessor within, the threshold of which was lowered to meet the new floor level. Subsequently, when the position of the entrance was altered this passage was filled in with a rough packing of rubble and mortar to a depth of about a metre in order to make a new floor level. When Traill erected his curtain wall the entrance was transferred and incorporated within this curtain wall. It was the arched opening now at the inner end of the present entrance passage; the northern wall, or inner wall of the range of buildings which the visitor passes through being then the curtain wall or outer wall of the castle. Subsequently, in front of this, a wall, the present front wall of the castle, was erected, extending from the Fore Tower to the great circular tower or Blockhouse at the south-west corner.

The Fore Tower was four storeys in height. It terminates in a rich corbel-table of two orders set chequer-wise and with a parapet-walk above. The walk does not continue all round but stops on the west side at the previous junction with the now vanished

6. *The south range and fore tower from the courtyard*

roof of the frontal range. On the east side it stops at the wall which ran across the interior. The two rooms divided by this cross-wall communicated one with another. The outer or southern was reached by steps leading down from the small east room of the frontal range. In both the tower rooms the reconstruction involved a raising of the floor levels. A vault was built to support the floor of the northern chamber. The floor of the southern chamber was raised on a bed of clay laid for the purpose.

The South Range

The ground floor of this frontal range consists of a vaulted chamber on either side of the entrance passage. Each contains a pit dug by the defenders of the castle while taking measures to countermine during the great siege of 1546–47. The end cross-wall of the east chamber clearly shows the junction of the original tower and the later extension of it. The end cross-wall of the western chamber is in reality the curved outer wall of the previously built circular Blockhouse referred to above, and the splayed aperture therein is a shot-hole of this tower designed to cover the curtain wall of Traill. The double-splayed basement courses of this wall can be clearly seen in each of these chambers. Above the ground floor apartments extended a long hall with access to the first floor of the Fore Tower and above this was a similar hall lit by characteristic Scots dormer windows. The dropped sills of these windows can be seen at the present wall-head.

The present entrance is corbelled out from the wall face and consists of an almost semi-circular moulded arch resting upon wall shafts with moulded caps and bases.

The area above the archway is divided horizontally by string-courses into panels of which the largest, directly above the arch, contains in the centre a panel-space probably intended for a coat-of-arms. Beneath it, faintly visible, is the date 1555. Above and across the panel runs a frieze of four circular labels each with a five-pointed star for Hamilton, the two central ones being framed together by round baluster mouldings, one on either side, continuing downward to frame the empty heraldic panel.[1]

To the east of the entrance there is a small door that probably served as a postern when the main gate was close. There is no evidence that this main gate was served by a drawbridge. References are made to a drawbridge in Cardinal Beaton's time but these apply to an earlier entrance. The stone pier in the ditch, which bears the footbridge today, had therefore a similar function in the early fifteenth century.

Passing through the inner arch at the end of the passage the visitor should remember that this is the entrance that existed before that which he has just passed under. Whereas his present further progress is in the open, while the castle was in use he would have continued through a further range of buildings, now vanished, before coming into the open light of the courtyard. Evidence of this other passage is still visible over the arched doorway of the courtyard.

The Blockhouse

In the south-west corner lies another curved segment of the ground floor of the great circular tower, or Blockhouse, as it was called, and a portion of the stair in it that served the upper chamber of the tower and southern range of buildings. This Blockhouse was one of the largest of its kind in Scotland, with a diameter of 16.2 m (53 ft). There was another Blockhouse at the corresponding south-east corner of which nothing now remains. According to Knox it was from the wall-head of this south-east tower that the murdered body of Cardinal Beaton was hung by two sheets for the edification and intimidation of the public, although tradition maintains that he was hung from the middle window of the Fore Tower. These two round towers of great size are good examples of a type which was common in parts of Europe in the early phase of the development of artillery fortifications. Continuing northwards the visitor will note the curtain wall on the west, and extending from it towards the courtyard a low continuous grass-covered mound indicating the possible existence of the foundations of the western range of buildings, probably storerooms, retainers' quarters, and stables. A diary kept by one of the garrison during the siege of 1547 reports the bombarding of the western range and the regrettable loss of a great quantity of wine thereby: 'the continuall schoting at the west partes of the castell spylte (spoiled) in our cellares and bruehouse one monthes provisiones'.

The Sea Tower and Bottle Dungeon

At the north-west corner stands the ruined Sea Tower, largely reconstructed in the sixteenth century. On the ground floor, which probably dates from the time of Traill, are two chambers. The eastern chamber was a prison cell without windows, ventilated by a narrow slot through the eastern wall. This slot was closed up by the insertion of vaulting at a later period. In the floor of the cell is a circular opening, the 'door' of the pit beneath, known as the 'Bottle Dungeon' on account of its shape. Hollowed out of the solid rock it is one of the most remarkable examples of the dark and incompassionate prisons found in most old Scottish castles. The depth of the pit is 7.3 m (24 ft) and it is

[1] The street front of St Mary's College, *circa* 1550, has a panel and surround of the same type. A striking parallel to both is a prominent feature of the Rosencrantz Tower in Bergen, 1562–63. It is difficult to parallel in Norway itself. But, in 1548, a Scot made a statue of St Hans for the rebuilding of the Greyfriars Church, Bergen, and in a list of artisans working in Bergen in 1558 a Scottish master mason is included. When Eric Rosencrantz rebuilt his tower he engaged builders and masons ('murmestre' and 'stenhuggere') from Scotland. These features have therefore an added significance. There is little doubt of Scottish influence in Bergen and every likelihood that the craftsmen who made the St Andrews panels were shortly afterwards at work there, continuing a well-established connection.

7. The courtyard and well, with remains of sea tower (left) and kitchen tower (right)

about 4.6 m (15 ft) wide at the bottom. 'In this place', says Knox, 'many of God's children were imprisoned'. Henry Forest; George Wishart, who was burnt outside the castle; John Roger, a black friar who was secretly murdered in its depths, and many others suffered for their religious faith or political opinion in this unwholesome pit.

The upper floor is mainly work of the sixteenth century and contains two chambers. The outer or eastern is a passage room with the remains of a re-used hooded fireplace of early type. Access to the floor above was by a wheel-stair projecting from the north wall. The inner apartment was vaulted and has windows to the south and west. In the north wall is a garderobe. The account of the siege of 1547 records that the French gunners 'schote doune all the battelyne and caiphouse of the seytowre and the hoyle ruffe of the chalmeris upone the partis of the sey', (shot down all the battlements and top-house of the sea-tower and the whole roof of the chambers overlooking the sea).

The North Range

Of this range only the outer wall remains. At the east end are the foundations of a circular oven inserted at a later date over what was probably a smaller oven or fuel hole. At the west end was a staircase rebuilt at the end of the sixteenth or in the seventeenth century.

There were 'chalmeris' (chambers) on the north side of the castle. These were probably the 'Gentilmenis chalmeris' referred to by Knox in his account of the murder of Cardinal Beaton.

Kitchen Tower

Of the Kitchen Tower little remains above two vaulted chambers dating from Bishop Traill's time. The kitchen was on the first floor and level with the hall of the east range. The fireplace has vanished but in the east kitchen wall are a slop-sink and two aumbries. The outer face of the tower has been strengthened in the sixteenth century

8. *The castle from the south-east*

by a massive buttress at the top of which appear two flues, probably from garderobes. A passage led to the north range, the opening at the outer end being probably a doorway to an access from cliff-steps. The vaulting of this passage is not original.

The East Range

From the Kitchen Tower extended the east range to meet the south or frontal ranges of the castle at the east Blockhouse in the south-east corner. Of this eastern range, once three storeys high, little can be said as nothing now remains but fragmentary parts of the inside wall of the ground floor, the building having vanished with the cliff it stood on. No doubt it contained a large dining hall served by the Kitchen Tower, with probably an open timber roof, and high windows looking across to the North Sea.

The Chapel Range

The southern ranges, facing the street, present the most important aspect of the castle and are most indicative of its former state. The Fore Tower should not be regarded as standing at the end of a building as it does today, but in the middle of two wings of equal size extending from it on either side at a slightly backward angle. The wing on the west has been described, that on the east was the chapel range, judging by an engraving by Slezer, done in 1718, when more existed than is evident today. On the ground floor were two chambers. The vaulting of these is not original, nor are the windows in the north wall. This opened on to a loggia with a north aspect – a feature of doubtful enjoyment anywhere in Scotland and particularly in St Andrews. Of this loggia only the bases of the columns exist today. The fireplace in the western gable is also a later insertion.

On the upper floor was the chapel. A jamb of one window remains, hollow-chamfered and grooved for glass. The drawing by Slezer shows two of the chapel windows complete and similar to those of the Chapel of St Leonard's College, which was built *c.* 1512. According to the drawing each is a double-light mullioned window with square lintel. Each light has quatrefoil tracery over a lancet daylight. The jambs of a third window are also indicated in the engraving. These chapel windows are more English than Scots in character.

9. *The Counter-mine*

The Mine and Counter-Mine

At the castle there is a very rare example of mediaeval siege technique, a mine and counter-mine tunnelled through the rock, dating from the siege of 1546–47. In 1546 it was reported to the French ambassador in London that 'The Governor, (ie, The Earl of Arran), had mined almost to the foot of the tower by which he hoped to capture it, although the defenders were counter-mining and showed no great fear'. As the Privy Council of Scotland resolved to the King of France to send hither twenty-four men skilled in the making and taking of fortifications, the mine and counter-mine, already in existence, are apparently of native workmanship. The besiegers started on the far side of the ditch to the south-east of the Fore Tower and drove a gallery 1.8 m (6 ft) wide and 2.1 m (7 ft) high (high enough for ponies to be used) towards the Fore Tower. The gallery sloped down to pass underneath the bottom of the ditch.

A mine head was made 8.2 m (27 ft) from the tower from which branches could be run, for the purpose no doubt of breaching the castle foundations at several places. But the work at this stage was abandoned for the defenders drove a counter-mine from the east of the Fore Tower to intercept the mine and broke through into the mine-head from a slightly higher level. The preliminary attempts of the garrison to estimate the course of the mine approaching on an unknown course to an unknown destination are recorded in the two trial pits excavated in the rock, one in each of the two chambers on either side of the entrance-passage. These attempts being given up the counter-mine was begun on the east of the Fore Tower and set at first an uncertain course towards the mine. The defenders, evidently still in doubt about its location, turned towards the east and drove a short gallery in this direction before they abandoned this work and resumed their original course which eventually carried them into the mine-head.

The entrance to the mine is beneath the modern house at the corner of Castle Wynd. The counter-mine is entered from within the castle precincts, at the south-east corner of the Fore Tower. From here the visitor can traverse both galleries in safety as the way is now floodlit with electric light. The quite remarkable size of the mine gallery will be noted, and the pick-marks of the sappers clearly seen. The coal seam, which is revealed in the Bottle Dungeon, is also evident.

10. *The Mine, showing the break-through by the counter-mine*

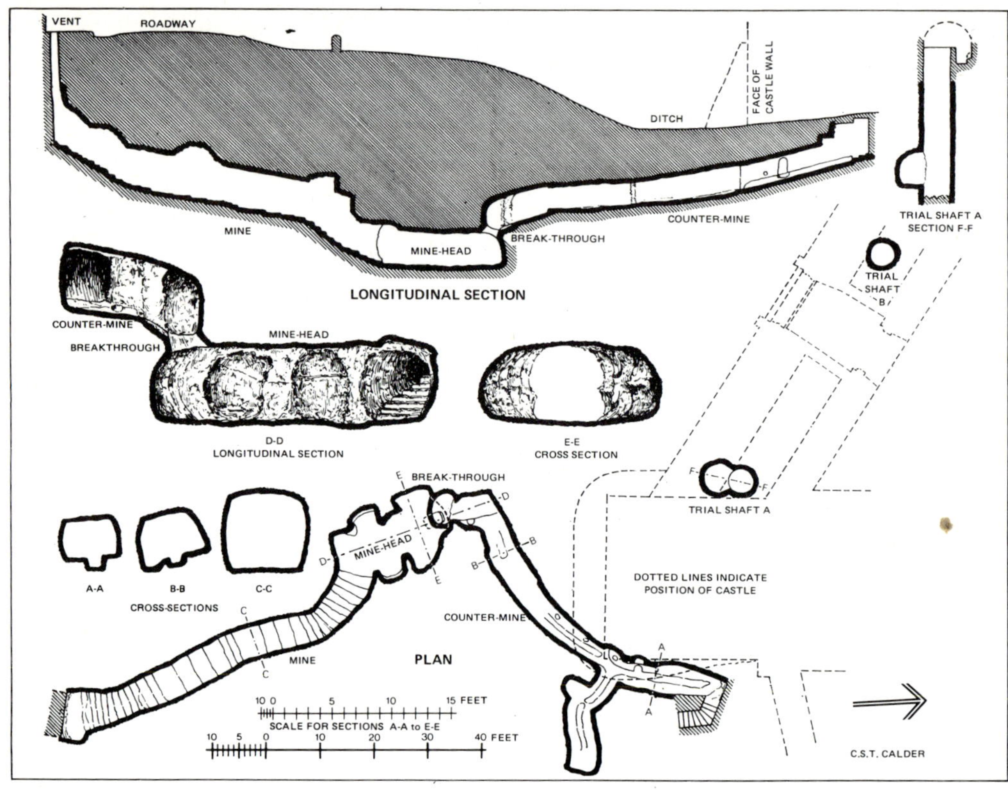

11. The mine and counter-mine

Glossary

Aumbry Small cupboard within a wall.
Chamfer The bevel or surface made by cutting away the angle.
Chases Grooves.
Cinquefoil A five-pointed leaf.
Corbel A projecting stone for the support of a timber beam or overhanging wall.
Cross-Loop An opening with arms, like a cross; usually for defence.
Curtain or *Curtain Wall* High enclosing wall.
Dropped Sills Decorative continuation of the window-sill below sill-level.
Gaff A timber beam from which the draw-bridge was suspended on chains.
Garderobe Mediaeval latrine.
Quatrefoil A four-pointed leaf.
Quoins Dressed corner stones.
Rebated Checked for door or window.
String Course Projecting moulding carried round the building.

Regnal Dates

John Balliol	1292–1296
The second Interregnum	1296–1306
Robert I (Bruce)	1306–1329
David II	1329–1371
Robert II (Stewart)	1370–1390
Robert III	1390–1406
James I	1406–1437
James II	1437–1460
James III	1460–1488
James IV	1488–1513
James V	1513–1542
Mary Queen of Scots	1542–1567
James VI	1567–1625
Edward I of England	1272–1307
Edward II of England	1307–1326
Edward III of England	1326–1377

Printed in Scotland for Her Majesty's Stationery Office by Alna Press Ltd., Broxburn. Dd. 630499/3404 C305 2/82.